SAINTLY RHYMES
FOR
modern times

WRITTEN AND ILLUSTRATED BY
MEGHAN BAUSCH

24 23 22 21 20   5 6 7 8 9 10 11

Our Sunday Visitor Publishing Division
Our Sunday Visitor, Inc.
200 Noll Plaza
Huntington, IN 46750
1-800-348-2440

ISBN: 978-1-68192-144-0 (Inventory No. T1866)
eISBN: 978-1-68192-146-4
LCCN: 2017948048

Cover design: Chelsea Alt
Cover art: Meghan Bausch
Interior design: Chelsea Alt
Interior art: Meghan Bausch

PRINTED IN THE UNITED STATES OF AMERICA

PRESENTED TO

_____

BY

_____

ON

_____

DEDICATED TO
OUR BLESSED MOTHER, MARY

Saint Thérèse
of
Lisieux

Saint Thérèse, the Little Flower,
shared her Little Way
of growing close to Jesus Christ
each and every day:

Kind words for someone grouchy,
a generous helping hand,
learning to smile and not complain
when things don't go as planned.

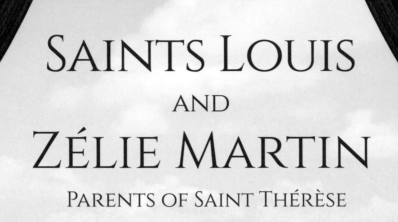

SAINTS LOUIS
AND
ZÉLIE MARTIN

PARENTS OF SAINT THÉRÈSE

Louis and Zélie show us
not all saints are priests or nuns.
Some are even dads and moms
who raise their little ones.

They taught their daughters prayers,
kissed their bruises when they fell,
and helped their youngest child
become a holy Saint as well!

SAINT MAXIMILIAN KOLBE

Saint Maximilian Kolbe
loved our Blessed Mother.
Like Jesus Christ, he sacrificed
his life to save another.

A man condemned to death cried out,
so Maximilian said,
"Please, sir, I am a Catholic priest.
I'll take his place instead."

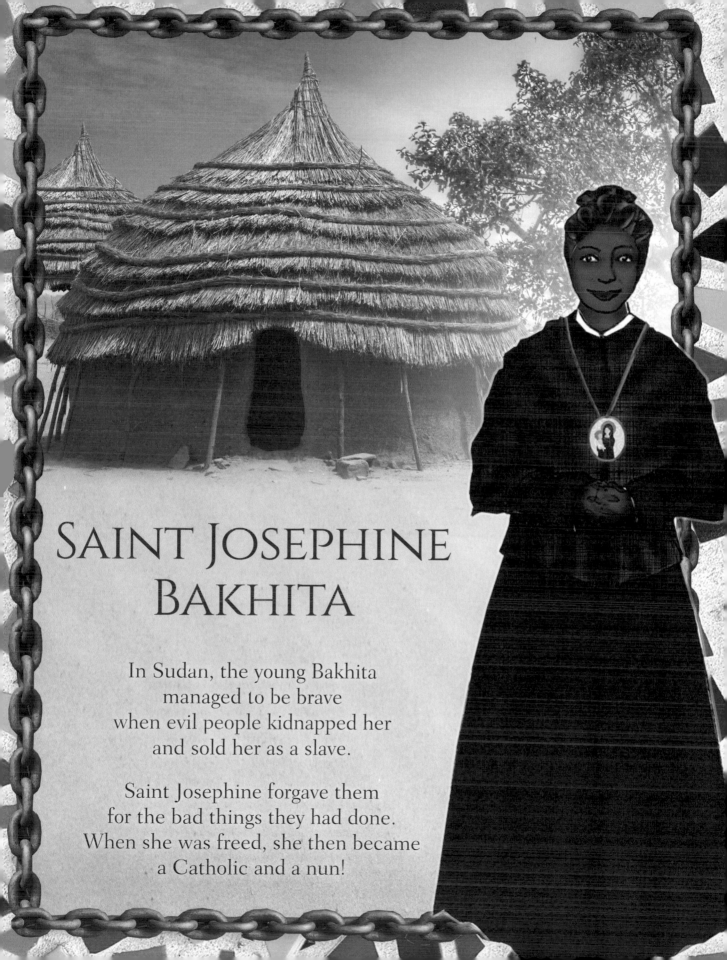

SAINT JOSEPHINE BAKHITA

In Sudan, the young Bakhita
managed to be brave
when evil people kidnapped her
and sold her as a slave.

Saint Josephine forgave them
for the bad things they had done.
When she was freed, she then became
a Catholic and a nun!

SAINT DAMIEN
OF
MOLOKAI

Saint Damien from Belgium
sailed across the seas
to serve and help Hawaiians
with a serious disease.

He dressed the wounds of people
whom others feared to touch;
built schools and homes, and told them,
"Jesus loves you very much!"

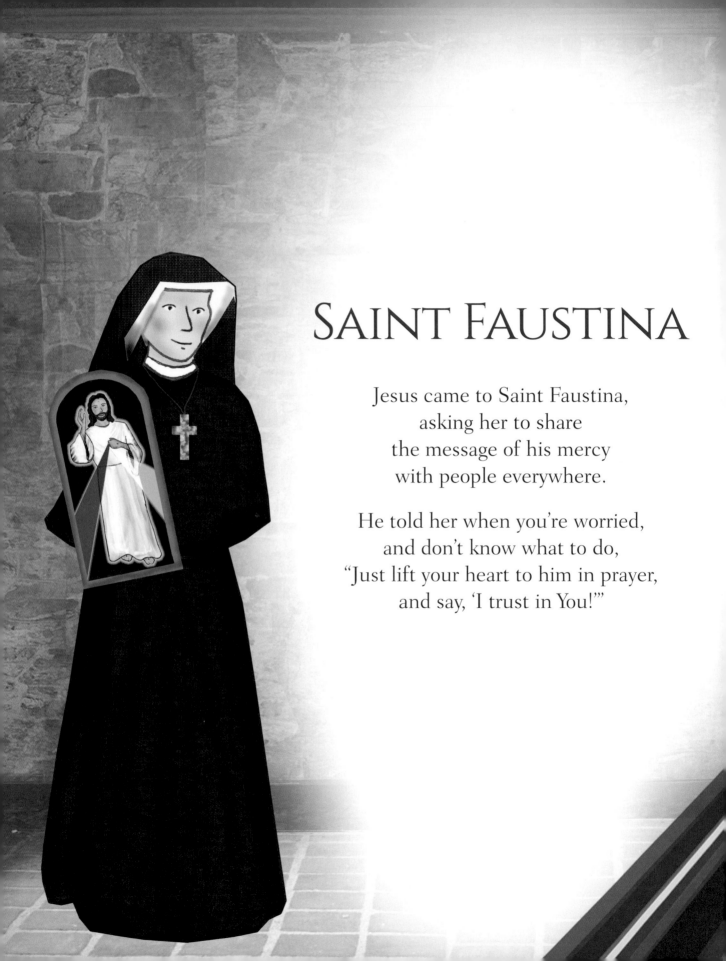

SAINT FAUSTINA

Jesus came to Saint Faustina,
asking her to share
the message of his mercy
with people everywhere.

He told her when you're worried,
and don't know what to do,
"Just lift your heart to him in prayer,
and say, 'I trust in You!'"

BLESSED
CHIARA "LUCE" BADANO

Chiara was a happy girl;
she sought to do God's will.
She lived her life in love and joy,
though she was very ill.

While sick in bed, she often said,
"My Jesus, just for you!
If this is what you want for me
then, Lord, I want it too!"

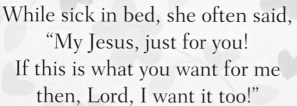

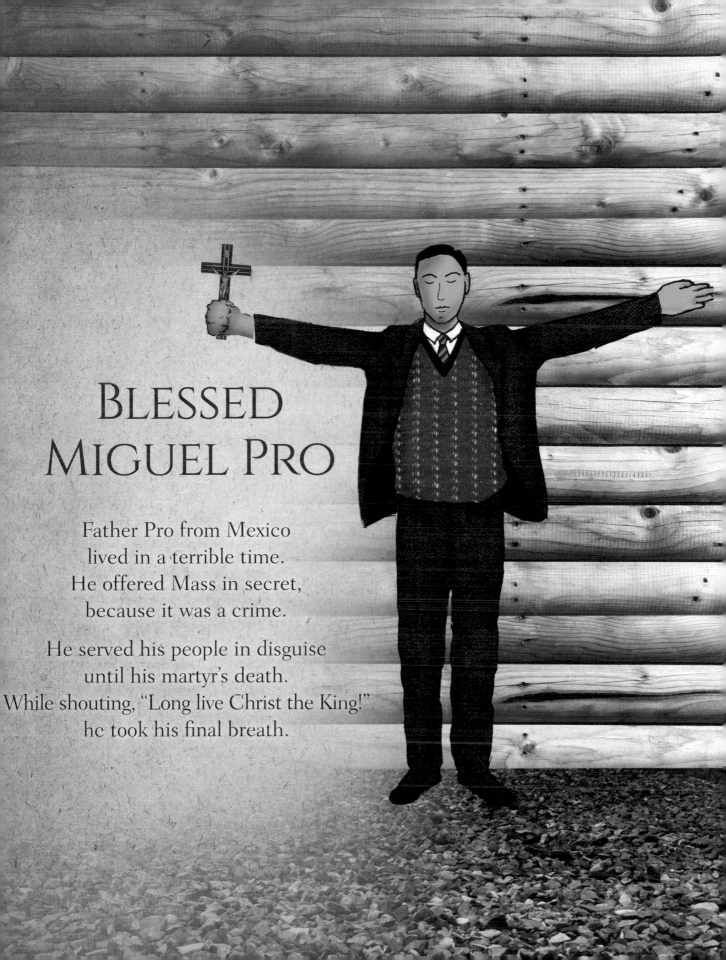

BLESSED MIGUEL PRO

Father Pro from Mexico
lived in a terrible time.
He offered Mass in secret,
because it was a crime.

He served his people in disguise
until his martyr's death.
While shouting, "Long live Christ the King!"
he took his final breath.

SAINT MOTHER TERESA

In India, Teresa
received a holy call
to help "the poorest of the poor"
in ways both great and small.

She loved those who were homeless,
hungry, orphaned, and ignored.
She showed that what we do for them
we do for Christ, Our Lord.

God gave Fulton Sheen
a very special mission:
to write a lot of books and host a show on television.

With smiles and jokes, he wrote and spoke
of what we gain by giving.
He often told both young and old that each life is worth living.

BLESSED PIER GIORGIO FRASSATI

Pier Giorgio Frassati
was cheerful, kind, and funny.
To friends in need, he gave away
his clothing, food, and money.

He lost himself for hours in prayer,
and worked hard at his studies.
He shared his faith on camping trips
with hiking and skiing buddies.

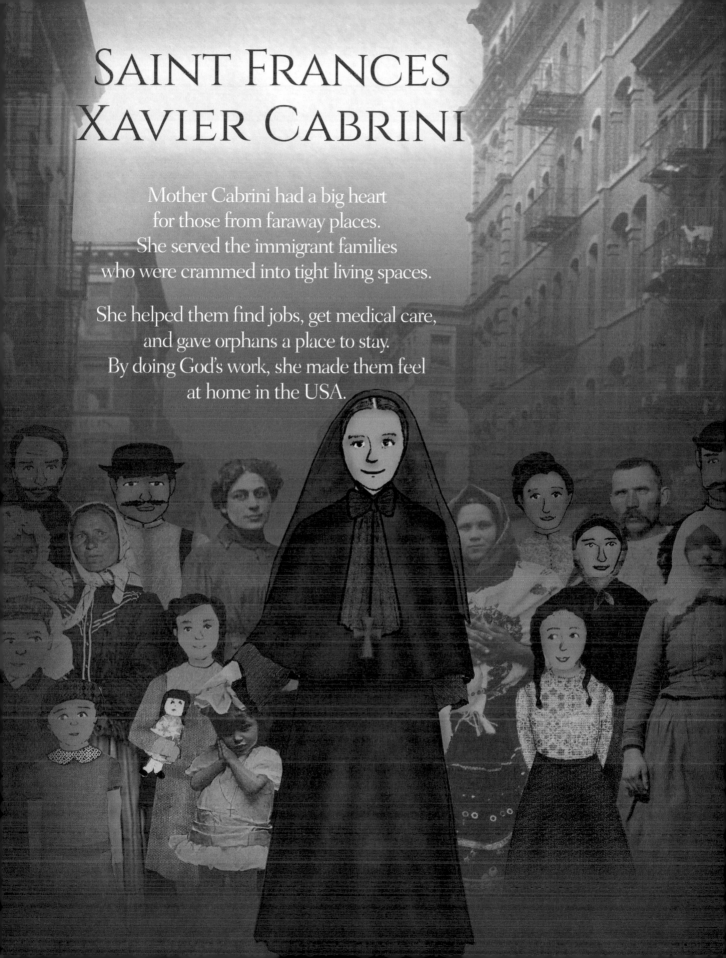

SAINT FRANCES XAVIER CABRINI

Mother Cabrini had a big heart
for those from faraway places.
She served the immigrant families
who were crammed into tight living spaces.

She helped them find jobs, get medical care,
and gave orphans a place to stay.
By doing God's work, she made them feel
at home in the USA.

Saint Gianna Beretta Molla

Holy Saint Gianna—
Doctor, Mother, Wife—
Showed us all the value
of every human life.

As a children's doctor,
she healed illnesses and hurts.
And as a loving mother,
she put her children first.

POPE SAINT JOHN PAUL II

Saint John Paul Two from Poland
was a poet and a pope.
His message was, "Be not afraid"
and "Do not give up hope."

He traveled to more countries
than any pope before.
When children cheered, "We love you!"
he replied, "I love you more!"

Saint Padre Pio

In the life of Padre Pio,
miracles abound.
He smelled like fragrant flowers
and could float above the ground!

He shared the wounds of Jesus,
heard confessions night and day.
He told us, "Never worry.
Just don't forget to pray!"

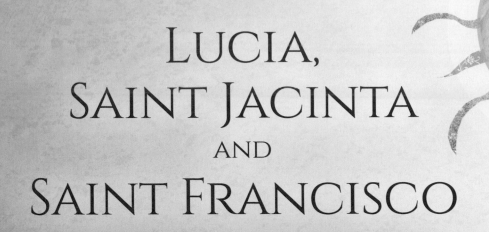

Lucia,
Saint Jacinta
and
Saint Francisco

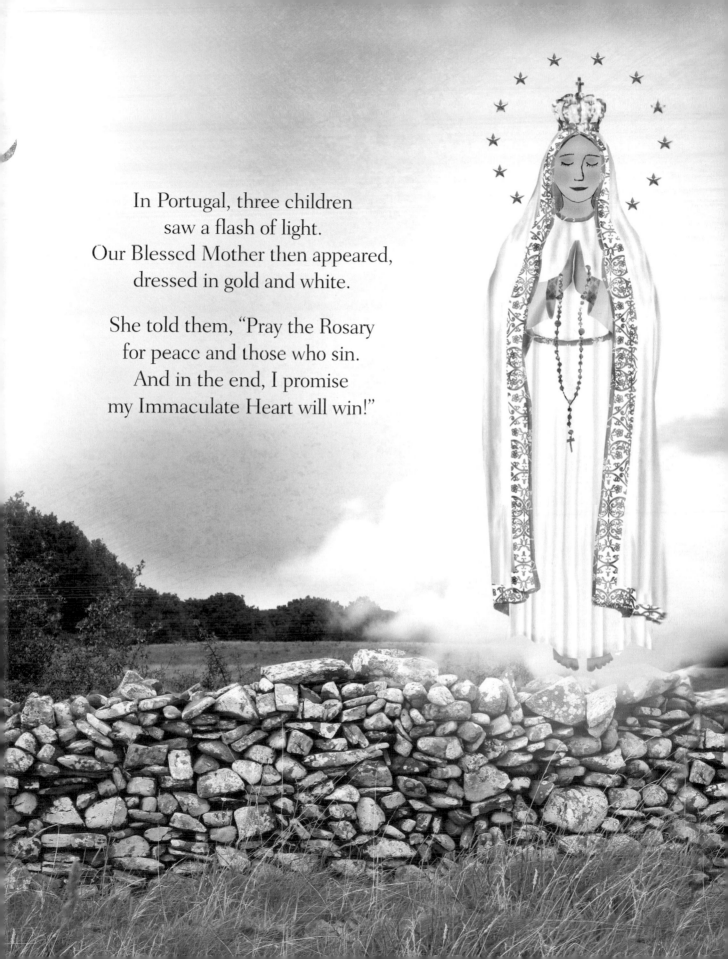

In Portugal, three children
saw a flash of light.
Our Blessed Mother then appeared,
dressed in gold and white.

She told them, "Pray the Rosary
for peace and those who sin.
And in the end, I promise
my Immaculate Heart will win!"